Our Five Senses

By Christian Lopetz

A Crabtree Seedlings Book

CRABTREE
Publishing Company
www.crabtreebooks.com

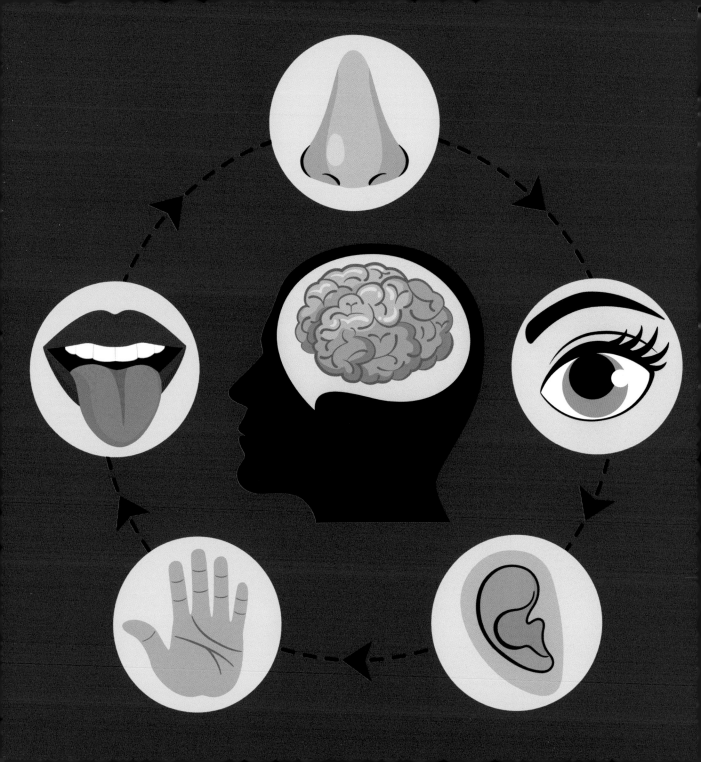

Table of Contents

Our Five Senses

We have five **senses**—seeing, hearing, smelling, tasting, and touching.

Our senses help us enjoy
the world around us.

Seeing

We use our eyes to see!

The black dot in the middle of your eye is called a **pupil**.

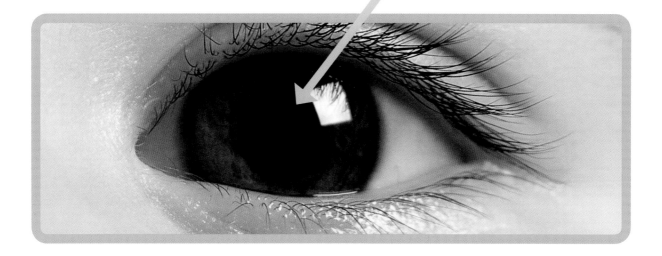

The pupil lets in light so you can see.

Sometimes we use our sight for fun, like reading a book or playing video games!

Other times we use our sight to stay safe.

Hearing

We hear with our ears.

Inside our ear we have an **eardrum**.

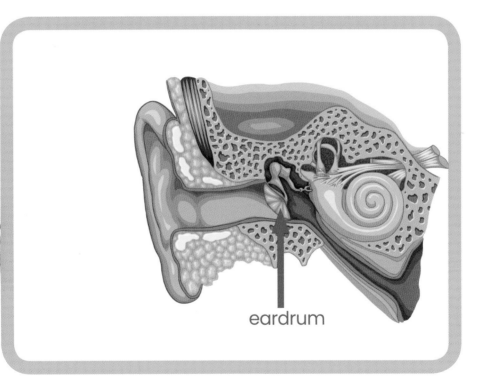

eardrum

Vibrations bounce off the eardrum and we hear sounds.

We use our hearing to enjoy music, or to listen to our teacher.

Smelling

We use our noses to smell.

Did you know that kids can smell things better than adults? As you get older, your sense of smell gets weaker.

We can use our nose to smell flowers.

We can use our nose to smell smoke in case there is a fire.

Tasting

We taste with our tongues.

Our tongues have **taste buds**.

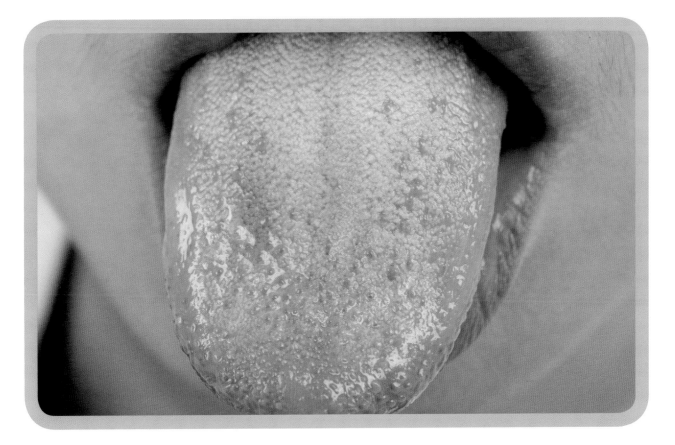

Taste buds tell us if something is sour, bitter, sweet, or salty.

We use the words sour, sweet, bitter, and salty to describe how something tastes.

sour

sweet

bitter

salty

Touching

Our skin gives us the sense of touch.

We have little **nerves** in our skin. These nerves let us feel pain.

These nerves can tell us if something is too hot.

We need our senses to stay safe, and to enjoy the world around us!

GLOSSARY

eardrum (EER-druhm): A membrane between the outer ear and middle ear that vibrates when struck by sound

nerves (NURVS): Thin fibers that carry messages between your brain and the rest of your body

pupil (PYOO-puhl): The black dot in the center of your eye that lets light in and allows you to see

senses (SENS-iz): Our ability to see, hear, taste, touch, and smell things

taste buds (TAYST buhdz): Little sensors on your tongue that allow you to taste food

vibrations (vye-BRAY-shunz): Very fast back and forth movements

INDEX:

School-to-Home Support for Caregivers and Teachers

This book helps children grow by letting them practice reading. Here are a few guiding questions to help the reader build his or her comprehension skills. Possible answers appear here in red.

Before Reading

- **What do I think this book is about?** *I think this book is about our five senses. I think this book is about smelling flowers.*

- **What do I want to learn about this topic?** *I want to learn more about my eyes and ears. I want to learn how my senses keep me safe.*

During Reading

- **I wonder why...** *I wonder why an eye's pupil is so small. I wonder why the eardrum is so deep in my ear.*

- **What have I learned so far?** *I have learned that the pupil of the eye lets in light so I can see. I have learned that there are little sensors on my tongue that allow me to taste food.*

After Reading

- **What details did I learn about this topic?** *I have learned that we have five senses that make it possible for us to see, hear, taste, touch, and smell things. I have learned that nerves are thin fibers that carry messages between our brain and the rest of our body.*

- **Read the book again and look for the glossary words.** *I see the word* **eardrum** *on page 11, and the words* **taste buds** *on page 19. The other glossary words are found on page 23.*

Library and Archives Canada Cataloguing in Publication

CIP available at Library and Archives Canada

Library of Congress Cataloging-in-Publication Data

CIP available at Library of Congress

Crabtree Publishing Company

www.crabtreebooks.com   1–800–387–7650

Written by Christian Lopetz

Print coordinator: Katherine Berti

Printed in the U.S.A./062021/CG20210401

Print book version produced jointly with Blue Door Education in 2022

Content produced and published by Blue Door Publishing LLC dba Blue Door Education, Melbourne Beach FL USA. Copyright Blue Door Publishing LLC. All rights reserved. No part of this book may be reproduced or utilized in any form or by any means, electronic or mechanical including photocopying, recording, or by any information storage and retrieval system without permission in writing from the publisher.

PHOTO CREDITS:
Cover © zhuda. Title: shutterstock.com/Hut Hanna. Page 4/5 © Dmitry Naumov, dainis, Arvind Balaraman, Anna Sedneva, zhuda. Page 6/7 © grublee, Yuliyan Velchev. Page 8/9 © Sean Prior, Sandra Gligorijevic. Page 10/11 © Masza$. Page 12/13 © Gelpi, Rob Marmion. Page 14 © Gelpi. Page 16/17 © Mark Payne, Vilant. Page 18/19 © Artur Gabrysiak, Arnold Reinhold. Page 20 © Sander Crombeen, Korovin Vitaly Anatolevich, Jaroslaw Grudzinski, Kenishirotie, page 21 © Xidong Luo, page 22 © Noam Armonn. All images from Shutterstock.com

Published in the United States
Crabtree Publishing
347 Fifth Ave.
Suite 1402-145
New York, NY 10016

Published in Canada
Crabtree Publishing
616 Welland Ave.
St. Catharines, Ontario
L2M 5V6